BOOK OF MERCY

BY LEONARD COHEN

Books

Let Us Compare Mythologies 1956

The Spice-Box of Earth 1961

The Favourite Game 1963

Flowers for Hitler 1964

Beautiful Losers 1966

Parasites of Heaven 1966

Selected Poems, 1956–1968 1968

The Energy of Slaves 1972

Death of a Lady's Man 1978

Book of Mercy 1984

Stranger Music 1993

Book of Longing 2006

Records

Songs of Leonard Cohen 1967

Songs from a Room 1969

Songs of Love and Hate 1971

Live Songs 1972

New Skin for the Old Ceremony 1973

The Best of Leonard Cohen 1975

Death of a Ladies' Man 1977

Recent Songs 1979

Various Positions 1984

I'm Your Man 1988

The Future 1992

Cohen Live 1994

More Best of Leonard Cohen 1997

Field Commander Cohen 2001

Ten New Songs 2001

The Essential Leonard Cohen 2002

Dear Heather 2004

Leonard Cohen

BOOK OF MERCY

McCLELLAND & STEWART

Library and Archives Canada Cataloguing in Publication

Cohen Leonard, 1934-
Book of mercy

Poems

ISBN 13: 978-0-7710-2182-4
ISBN 10: 0-7710-2182-8 (PBK)
ISBN 10: 0-7710-2206-9 (BOUND)

I. Title.

PS8505.044B66 1984   C811'.54   C84-098238-0
PR9199.3.C62B66 1984

We acknowledge the financial support of the Government of Canada through the Book Publishing Industry Development Program and that of the Government of Ontario through the Ontario Media Development Corporation's Ontario Book Initiative. We further acknowledge the support of the Canada Council for the Arts and the Ontario Arts Council for our publishing program.

Set in Perpetua by The Typeworks, Vancouver
Printed and bound in Canada

McClelland & Stewart Ltd.
75 Sherbourne Street
Toronto, Ontario
M5A 2P9
www.mcclelland.com

9 10 11   10 09

for my teacher

I

I

I STOPPED TO LISTEN, BUT he did not come. I began again with a sense of loss. As this sense deepened I heard him again. I stopped stopping and I stopped starting, and I allowed myself to be crushed by ignorance. This was a strategy, and didn't work at all. Much time, years were wasted in such a minor mode. I bargain now. I offer buttons for his love. I beg for mercy. Slowly he yields. Haltingly he moves toward his throne. Reluctantly the angels grant to one another permission to sing. In a transition so delicate it cannot be marked, the court is established on beams of golden symmetry, and once again I am a singer in the lower choirs, born fifty years ago to raise my voice this high, and no higher.

2

WHEN I LEFT THE KING I began to rehearse what I would say to the world: long rehearsals full of revisions, imaginary applause, humiliations, edicts of revenge. I grew swollen as I conspired with my ambition, I struggled, I expanded, and when the term was up, I gave birth to an ape. After some small inevitable misunderstanding, the ape turned on me. Limping, stumbling, I fled back to the swept courtyards of the king. 'Where is your ape?' the king demanded. 'Bring me your ape.' The work is slow. The ape is old. He clowns behind his bars, imitating our hands in the dream. He winks at my official sense of urgency. What king, he wants to know. What courtyard? What highway?

3

I HEARD MY SOUL SINGING
behind a leaf, plucked the leaf, but then I heard it sing-
ing behind a veil. I tore the veil, but then I heard it sing-
ing behind a wall. I broke the wall, and I heard my soul
singing against me. I built up the wall, mended the cur-
tain, but I could not put back the leaf. I held it in my
hand and I heard my soul singing mightily against me.
This is what it's like to study without a friend.

4

AFTER SEARCHING AMONG the words, and never finding ease, I went to you, I asked you to gladden my heart. My prayer divided against itself, I was ashamed to have been deceived again, and bitterly, in the midst of loud defeat, I went out myself to gladden the heart. It was here that I found my will, a fragile thing, starving among ferns and women and snakes. I said to my will, 'Come, let us make ourselves ready to be touched by the angel of song,' and suddenly I was once again on the bed of defeat in the middle of the night, begging for mercy, searching among the words. With the two shields of bitterness and hope, I rose up carefully, and I went out of the house to rescue the angel of song from the place where she had chained herself to her nakedness. I covered her nakedness with my will, and we stood in the kingdom that shines toward you, where Adam is mysteriously free, and I searched among the words for words that would not bend the will away from you.

5

'LET ME REST,' HE CRIED from the panic at the top of his heap of days. 'Let me rest on the day of rest,' he entreated from the throne of unemployment. 'This king is heavy in my arms, I can't hold up the Pharaoh any more.' He fastened his collar to the darkness so he couldn't breathe, and he opened the book in anger to make his payment to the law. An angel, who had no intrinsic authority, said, 'You have sealed every gate but this one; therefore, here is a little light commensurate with your little courage.' His shame climbed up itself to find a height from which to spill. Then there was a sweeter saying in a stiller voice: 'I do not put my trust in man, nor do I place reliance on an angel.' Immediately the Torah sang to him, and touched his hair, and for a moment, as a gift to serve his oldest memory, he wore the weightless crown, the crown that lifts the weight away, he wore it till his heart could say, 'How precious is the heritage!' The crown that leaps up from the letters, a crown like dew that gives the grass to drink beads out of the darkness, the mother's kiss at the beginning of the war, the father's hand that lets the forehead shine, the crown that raises up no man a king above his company. 'Lead me deep into your Sabbath, let me sit beneath the mighty ones whom you have crowned forever, and let me study how they rest.'

6

SIT DOWN, MASTER, ON
this rude chair of praises, and rule my nervous heart
with your great decrees of freedom. Out of time you
have taken me to do my daily task. Out of mist and dust
you have fashioned me to know the numberless worlds
between the crown and the kingdom. In utter defeat I
came to you and you received me with a sweetness I
had not dared to remember. Tonight I come to you
again, soiled by strategies and trapped in the loneliness
of my tiny domain. Establish your law in this walled
place. Let nine men come to lift me into their prayer so
that I may whisper with them: Blessed be the name of
the glory of the kingdom forever and forever.

7

I PUSHED MY BODY FROM one city to another, one rooftop to another, to see a woman bathing. I heard myself grunt. I saw my fingers glisten. Then the exile closed around me. Then the punishment began; a small aimless misery, not in the heart, in the throat, then the removal of the body, the birds singing to a treasure of garbage, then world amnesia, a ghost bathing and shitting. Then I was judged by the face of one I tricked. Then the fear of justice. Then, for the ten thousandth time, the reality of sin. Then the Law shining, then the memory of what it was, too far, too clean to be grasped. Then I longed to long for you again, to know the ache of separation. How long must I be uninhabited by a soul? How long sustain the mutiny of this denial? O master of my breath, create a man around these nostrils, and gather my heart toward the gravity of your name. Form me again with an utterance and open my mouth with your praise. There is no life but in affirming you, no world to walk on but the one which you create. Forgive me with these hours and this midnight. Give this thought a master, and this ghost a stone. And do not let the demons boast about your mercy.

8

IN THE EYES OF MEN HE falls, and in his own eyes too. He falls from his high place, he trips on his achievement. He falls to you, he falls to know you. It is sad, they say. See his disgrace, say the ones at his heel. But he falls radiantly toward the light to which he falls. They cannot see who lifts him as he falls, or how his falling changes, and he himself bewildered till his heart cries out to bless the one who holds him in his falling. And in his fall he hears his heart cry out, his heart explains why he is falling, why he had to fall, and he gives over to the fall. Blessed are you, clasp of the falling. He falls into the sky, he falls into the light, none can hurt him as he falls. Blessed are you, shield of the falling. Wrapped in his fall, concealed within his fall, he finds the place, he is gathered in. While his hair streams back and his clothes tear in the wind, he is held up, comforted, he enters into the place of his fall. Blessed are you, embrace of the falling, foundation of the light, master of the human accident.

9

Blessed are you who has given each man a shield of loneliness so that he cannot forget you. You are the truth of loneliness, and only your name addresses it. Strengthen my loneliness that I may be healed in your name, which is beyond all consolations that are uttered on this earth. Only in your name can I stand in the rush of time, only when this loneliness is yours can I lift my sins toward your mercy.

10

You have sweetened your word on my lips. My son too has heard the song that does not belong to him. From Abraham to Augustine, the nations have not known you, though every cry, every curse is raised on the foundation of your holiness. You placed me in this mystery and you let me sing, though only from this curious corner. You bound me to my fingerprints, as you bind every man, except the ones who need no binding. You led me to this field where I can dance with a broken knee. You led me safely to this night, you gave me a crown of darkness and light, and tears to greet my enemy. Who can tell of your glory, who can number your forms, who dares expound the interior life of god? And now you feed my household, you gather them to sleep, to dream, to dream freely, you surround them with the fence of all that I have seen. Sleep, my son, my small daughter, sleep – this night, this mercy has no boundaries.

II

He CAME BACK FROM HIS prayer to the cat on his lap. He fed the cat, he let her go out to the moonlight, and he hid in the pages of Abraham. Like one newly circumcized, he hid himself away, he waited in the trust of healing. Faces of women appeared, and they explained themselves to him, connecting feature to character, beauty to kindness. Various families came to him and showed him all the chairs he might sit in. 'How can I say this gently?' he said. 'Though I love your company, your instructions are wasted here. I will always choose the woman who carries me off, I will always sit with the family of loneliness.' Saying many words of encouragement his visitors departed, and he entered more deeply into his hiding. He asked for his heart to be focused toward the source of mercy, and he lifted up a corner, and he moved a millimetre forward under the shadow of the tabernacle of peace. His cat came back from the moonlight, flew softly to her place on his lap, and waited for him to come back from his prayer.

12

I DRAW ASIDE THE CUR-
tain. You mock us with the beauty of your world. My
heart hates the trees, the wind moving the branches,
the dead diamond machinery of the sky. I pace the cor-
ridor between my teeth and my bladder, angry, mur-
derous, comforted by the smell of my sweat. I weak-
ened myself in your name. In my own eyes I disgraced
myself for trusting you, against all evidence, against the
prevailing winds of horror, over the bully's laughter,
the torturer's loyalty, the sweet questions of the sly.
Find me here, you whom David found in hell. The

skeletons are waiting for your famous mechanical salvation. Swim through the blood, father of mercy. Broadcast your light through the apple of pain, radiant one, sourceless, source of light. I wait for you, king of the dead, here in this garden where you placed me, beside the poisonous grass, miasmal homesteads, black Hebrew gibberish of pruned grapevines. I wait for you in the springtime of beatings and gross unnecessary death. Direct me out of this, O magnet of the falling cherry petals. Make a truce between my disgust and the impeccable landscape of fields and milky towns. Crush my swollen smallness, infiltrate my shame. Broken in the unemployment of my soul, I have driven a wedge into your world, fallen on both sides of it. Count me back to your mercy with the measures of a bitter song, and do not separate me from my tears.

13

FRIEND, WHEN YOU SPEAK this carefully I know it is because you don't know what to say. I listen in such a way so as not to add to your confusion. I make some reply at every opportunity so as not to compound your loneliness. Thus the conversation continues under an umbrella of optimism. If you suggest a feeling, I affirm it. If you provoke, I accept the challenge. The surface is thick, but it has its flaws, and hopefully we will trip on one of them. Now, we can order a meat sandwich for the protein, or we can take our places in the Sanhedrin and determine what is to be done with those great cubes of diamond that our teacher Moses shouldered down the mountain. You want to place them in such a way that the sun by day, and the moon and stars by night, will shine through them. I suggest another perspective which would include the light of the celestial bodies within the supernal radiance of the cubes. We lean toward each other over the table. The dust mingles with the mist, our nostrils widen. We are definitely interested; now we can get down to a Jew's business.

14

BLESSED ARE YOU WHO, among the numberless swept away in terror, permitted a few to suffer carefully. Who put a curtain over a house so that a few could lower their eyes. Blessed be Ishmael, who taught us how to cover ourselves. Blessed are you who dressed the shivering spirit in a skin. Who made a fence of changing stars around your wisdom. Blessed be the teacher of my heart, on his throne of patience. Blessed are you who circled desire with a blade, and the garden with fiery swords, and heaven and earth with a word. Who, in the terrible inferno, sheltered understanding, and keeps her still, beautiful and deeply concealed. Blessed are you who sweetens the longing between us. Blessed are you who binds the arm to the heart, and the will to the will. Who has written a name on a gate, that she might find it, and come into my room. Who defends a heart with strangerhood. Blessed are you who sealed a house with weeping. Blessed be Ishmael for all time, who covered his face with the wilderness, and came to you in darkness. Blessed be the covenant of love between what is hidden and what is revealed. I was like one who had never been caressed, when you touched me from a place in your name, and dressed the wound of ignorance with mercy. Blessed is the covenant of love, the covenant of mercy, useless light behind the terror, deathless song in the house of night.

Ishmael, first son of Abraham and his hand-maiden Hagar, is traditionally considered the father of the Arab nation.

15

THIS IS THE WAY WE SUM-
mon one another, but it is not the way we call upon the
Name. We stand in rags, we beg for tears to dissolve
the immovable landmarks of hatred. How beautiful our
heritage, to have this way of speaking to eternity, how
bountiful this solitude, surrounded, filled, and mas-
tered by the Name, from which all things arise in splen-
dour, depending one upon the other.

16

Return, spirit, to this lowly place. Come down. There is no path where you project yourself. Come down; from here you can look at the sky. From here you can begin to climb. Draw back your song from the middle air where you cannot follow it. Close down these shaking towers you have built toward your vertigo. You do not know how to bind your heart to the skylark, or your eyes to the hardened blue hills. Return to the sorrow in which you have hidden your truth. Kneel here, search here, with both hands, the cat's cradle of your tiny distress. Listen to the one who has not been wounded, the one who says, 'It is not good that man should be alone.' Recall your longing to the loneliness where it was born, so that when she appears, she will stand before you, not against you. Refine your longing here, in the small silver music of her preparations, under the low-built shelter of repentance.

17

 D ID WE COME FOR NOTH-
ing? We thought we were summoned, the aging head-
waiters, the minor singers, the second-rate priests. But
we couldn't escape into these self-descriptions, nor
lose ourselves in the atlas of coming and going. Our
prayer is like gossip, our work like burning grass. The
teacher is pushed over, the bird-watcher makes a noise,
and the madman dares himself to be born into the ques-
tion of who he is. Let the light catch the thread from

which the man is hanging. Heal him inside the wind, wrap the wind around his broken ribs, you who know where Egypt was, and for whom he rehearses these sorrows, Our Lady of the Torah, who does not write history, but whose kind lips are the law of all activity. How strangely you prepare his soul. The heretic lies down beside the connoisseur of form, the creature of desire sits on a silver ring, the counterfeiter begs forgiveness from the better counterfeiter, the Angel of Darkness explains the difference between a palace and a cave – O bridge of silk, O single strand of spittle glistening, a hair of possibility, and nothing works, nothing works but You.

18

THEY KNOW ME AT THIS café. When I come in from the vineyards they put a drink in front of me. As a sign of respect I take off my sunglasses whenever I speak to the proprietress. Here I can reflect on the Romans, their triumph, and the tiny thorn in their side that we represent. The owners are exiles too, scattered people, as are their customers, who all seem to wear dark suits and flash gold teeth behind their cigarette-holders. Our children go to the Roman schools. We drink coffee, and some kind of powerful fruit brandy, and we hope that the grand-children will return to us. Our hope is in the distant seed. Occasionally the card-players in the corner lift little glasses in a toast, and I lift mine, joining them in their incomprehensible affirmation. The cards fly between their fingers and the mica table-top, old cards, so familiar they hardly have to turn them over to see who has won the hand. Take heart, you who were born in the captivity of a fixed predicament; and tremble, you kings of certainty: your iron has become like glass, and the word has been uttered that will shatter it.

19

YOU LET ME SING, YOU
lifted me up, you gave my soul a beam to travel on. You
folded your distance back into my heart. You drew the
tears back to my eyes. You hid me in the mountain of
your word. You gave the injury a tongue to heal itself.
You covered my head with my teacher's care, you
bound my arm with my grandfather's strength. O be-
loved speaking, O comfort whispering in the terror, un-
speakable explanation of the smoke and cruelty, undo
the self-conspiracy, let me dare the boldness of joy.

20

LIKE AN UNBORN INFANT swimming to be born, like a woman counting breath in the spasms of labour, I yearn for you. Like a fish pulled to the minnow, the angler to the point of line and water, I am fixed in a strict demand, O king of absolute unity. What must I do to sweeten this expectancy, to rescue hope from the scorn of my enemy? The child is born into your world, the fish is fed and the fisherman too. Bathsheba lies with David, apes come down from the Tower of Babel, but in my heart an ape sees the beauty bathing. From every side of Hell is my greed affirmed. O shield of Abraham, affirm my hopefulness.

21

My teacher gave me what I do not need, told me what I need not know. At a high price he sold me water beside the river. In the middle of a dream he led me gently to my bed. He threw me out when I was crawling, took me in when I was home. He referred me to the crickets when I had to sing, and when I tried to be alone he fastened me to a congregation. He curled his fists and pounded me toward my proper shape. He puked in disgust when I swelled without filling. He sank his tiger teeth into everything of mine that I refused to claim. He drove me through the pine trees at an incredible speed to that realm where I barked with a dog, slid with the shadows, and leaped from a point of view. He let me be a student of a love that I will never be able to give. He suffered me to play at friendship with my truest friend. When he was certain that I was incapable of self-reform, he flung me across the fence of the Torah.

22

YOUR CUNNING CHARLA-
tan is trying to whip up a frisson of grace. He wants a
free ride and a little on the side. He has hid his shame
under a tired animal gleam, and he pretends to be full
of health. He's working hard, dragging that donkey up
Mount Moriah. And listen to the authentic muffled cry
of his heart, so thoroughly documented and unat-
tended. He has some pictures in his mind, they're all
round and wet, very pressing, and he has his belt, he's
going to give her what she wants. Bring a mirror, let
him see the monkey struggling with the black tefillin
straps. Where is she, Lord of Unity, where is the kind
face, the midnight help, the autumn wedding, the wed-
ding with no blood?

23

My sister and i being estranged, I parked my trailer at the furthest limit of her fields, the corner that is left, by law, to the poor. Her hundreds of cherry trees were blossoming, and on the road to the great stone house that they lined, a lacework of petals. It was a Saturday. I reclined against a little hill, a shoot of wheat between my teeth, looked at the blue sky, a bird, three threads of luminous cloud, and my heart would not rejoice. I entered the hour of self-accusation. A strange sound trembled in the air. It was caused by the north wind on the electric lines, a sustained chord of surprising harmonies, power and duration, greatly pleasing, a singing of breath and steel, a huge string instrument of masts and fields, complex tensions. Suddenly the judgement was clear. Let your sister, with her towers and gardens, praise the incomparable handiwork of the Lord, but you are pledged to the breath of the Name. Each of you in your proper place. The cherry trees are hers, the grapes and the olives, the thick-walled house; and to you, the unimagined charities of accident in the Corner of the Poor.

24

IN THE THIN LIGHT OF
hunted pleasure, I become afraid that I will never know
my sorrow. I call on you with a cry that concentrates
the heart. When will I cry out in gratitude? When will I
sing to your mercy? Tomorrow is yours, the past is in
debt, and death runs toward me with the soiled white
flag of surrender. O draw me out of an easy skill into
the art of the holy. I am afraid of what I have done to
my soul, and the judgement is established like a sudden
noise. O help me bow down to your anger. I lie beside
the corpse of my idol, in the spell of fire and ashes, my
word for the day of atonement forgotten. Lift me up
with a new heart, with an old memory, for my father's

sake, for the sake of your name which rings in heaven and hell, through worlds destroyed and worlds to come, tangible music shining between the hidden and the perceived, garbled in my ear and clearly the place I stand on, O precious name of truth uncontradicting. The scornful man will bend his knee, and holy souls will be drawn down into his house. Hedges will be planted in the rotting world, the young shoots protected. Time will be measured from mother to child, from father to son, and learning will speak to learning. Even the evil are weary, the bomb falls on the pilot's son, the riot shouts out to be calmed. The wound widens every heart, the general exile thickens, the whole world becomes the memory of your absence. How long will you hunt us with sorrow? How long will they rage, the fires of refinement? Blood drinking blood, wound swallowing wound, sorrow torturing sorrow, cruelty rehearsing itself under the measureless night of your patience. When will the work of truth begin, to verify your promise? Now that all men hear each other, let your name be established in hell, and count us back to the safety of your law, father of mercy, bride of the captured earth. Speak to your child of his healing, in this place where we are for a moment.

25

My son and i lived in a cave for many years, hiding from the Romans, the Christians, and the apostate Jews. Night and day we studied the letters of one word. When one of us grew tired, the other would urge him on. One morning he said, 'I've had enough,' and I said 'I agree.' He married a beautiful girl, the daughter of one of our benefactors, grown from the child who brought us food in the night to the one for whom he waited all day, and they were blessed with children. My wife came back to me one strange afternoon, all changed, all lightened, and we opened a bookstall in Jerusalem, where we sold small bilingual editions of the Book of Psalms. My daughter appeared one day and said, 'I believe you have neglected me.' 'Forgive me,' I said, and her face shone with forgiveness. She married a goldsmith, a maker of ceremonial objects, bore children, and deepened the happiness of her parents. Every so often we gather at midnight before the Wall, our family of little families. 'After all,' we say, 'the Romans do not eat flesh torn from a living animal, and the Christians are a branch of the tree, and the apostate Jews are still embraced by the Word.' We talk in this manner, we sing the time-honoured songs, and we compose new ones, as we were commanded:

> *Jerusalem of blood*
> *Jerusalem of amnesia*
> *Jerusalem of idolatry*
> *Jerusalem of Washington*
> *Jerusalem of Moscow*
> *Let the nations rejoice*
> *Jerusalem has been destroyed*

26

Sit in a chair and keep still. Let the dancer's shoulders emerge from your shoulders, the dancer's chest from your chest, the dancer's loins from your loins, the dancer's hips and thighs from yours; and from your silence the throat that makes a sound, and from your bafflement a clear song to which the dancer moves, and let him serve God in beauty. When he fails, send him again from your chair. By such an exercise, even a bitter man can praise Creation, even a heavy man can swoon, and a man of high responsibility soften his heart.

II

27

ISRAEL, AND YOU WHO call yourself Israel, the Church that calls itself Israel, and the revolt that calls itself Israel, and every nation chosen to be a nation – none of these lands is yours, all of you are thieves of holiness, all of you at war with Mercy. Who will say it? Will America say, We have stolen it, or France step down? Will Russia confess, or Poland say, We have sinned? All bloated on their scraps of destiny, all swaggering in the immunity of superstition. Ishmael, who was saved in the wilderness, and given shade in the desert, and a deadly treasure under you: has Mercy made you wise? Will Ishmael declare, We are in debt forever? Therefore the lands belong to none of you, the borders do not hold, the Law will never serve the lawless. To every people the land is given on condition. Perceived or not, there is a Covenant, beyond the constitution, beyond sovereign guarantee, beyond the nation's sweetest dreams of itself. The Covenant is broken, the condition is dishonoured, have you not noticed that the world has been taken away? You have no place, you will wander through yourselves from generation to generation without a thread. Therefore you rule over chaos, you hoist your flags with no authority, and the heart that is still alive hates you, and the remnant of Mercy is ashamed to look at you. You decompose behind your flimsy armour, your stench alarms you, your panic strikes at love. The land is not yours, the land has been taken back, your shrines fall through empty air, your tablets are quickly revised, and you bow down in hell beside your hired torturers, and still you count your battalions and crank out your marching songs. Your righteous enemy is listening. He hears your anthems full of blood and vanity, and your children singing to themselves. He has overturned the vehicle of nationhood, he has spilled the precious cargo, and every nation he has taken back. Because you are swollen with your little time. Because you do not wrestle with your angel. Because you dare to live without God. Because your cowardice has led you to believe that the victor does not limp.

28

You who pour mercy in-
to hell, sole authority in the highest and the lowest
worlds, let your anger disperse the mist in this aimless
place, where even my sins fall short of the mark. Let me
be with you again, absolute companion, let me study
your ways which are just beyond the hope of evil. Seize
my heart out of its fantasy, direct my heart from the
fiction of secrecy, you who know the secrets of every

heart, whose mercy is to be the secret of longing. Let every heart declare its secret, let every song disclose your love, let us bring to you the sorrows of our freedom. Blessed are you, who opens a gate in every moment, to enter in truth or tarry in hell. Let me be with you again, let me put this away, you who wait beside me, who have broken down your world to gather hearts. Blessed is your name, blessed is the confession of your name. Kindle the darkness of my calling, let me cry to the one who judges the heart in justice and mercy. Arouse my heart again with the limitless breath you breathe into me, arouse the secret from obscurity.

29

Bless the lord, o my soul, who made you a singer in his holy house forever, who has given you a tongue like the wind, and a heart like the sea, who has journeyed you from generation to generation to this impeccable moment of sweet bewilderment. Bless the Lord who has surrounded the traffic of human interest with the majesty of his law, who has given a direction to the falling leaf, and a goal to the green shoot. Tremble, my soul, before the one who creates good and evil, that a man may choose among worlds; and tremble before the furnace of light in which you are formed and to which you return, until the time when he suspends his light and withdraws into himself, and there is no world, and there is no soul anywhere. Bless the one who judges you with his strap and his mercy, who covers with a million years of dust those who say, I have not sinned. Gather me, O my soul, around your longing, and from your eternal place inform my homelessness, that I may bring you forth and husband you, and make the day a throne for your activity, and the night a tower for your watchfulness, and all my time your just dominion. Sing, my soul, to the one who moves like music, who comes down like steps of lightning, who widens space with the thought of his name, who returns like death, deep and intangible, to his own absence and his own glory. Bless the Lord, O my soul, draw down the blessing of authority, that you may invite me to uncover you, and hold you precious till I'm worn away, and we are refreshed, soul and shadow, refreshed and rested like a sundial standing in the night. Bless the Lord, O my soul, cry out toward his mercy, cry out with tears and song and every instrument, stretch yourself toward the undivided glory which he established merely as his footstool, when he created forever, and he made it-is-finished, and he signed the foundations of unity, and polished the atoms of love to shine back beams and paths and gates of return. Bless the Lord, O my soul. Bless his name forever.

30

H ERE THE DESTRUCTION is subtle, and there the body is torn. Here the breaking is perceived, and there the dead unaware carry their putrid remains. All trade in filth, carry their filth one to another, all walk the streets as though the ground did not recoil, all stretch their necks to bite the air, as though the breath had not withdrawn. The seed bursts without a blessing, and the harvest is gathered as if it were food. The bride and the bridegroom sink down to combine, and flesh is brought forth as if it were child. They bring their unclean hands to secret doctors, amazed at their pain, as if they had washed their hands, as if they had lifted up their hands. They write and they weep, as though evil were the miracle. They hear bad tidings, as though they were the judge. They run to what they have not soiled, but the trees and waters hide themselves behind a blessing which they are too proud to know. What they kill is already dead, and what they eat, though it be the wildest berry and they suck it from the stem, has withered long before. Let them lie on the grass, they lie on a machine. There is no world without the blessing, and every plate to which they drop their face is an abomination of blood and suffering and maggots. They leap on the hunchback with a knife, they tear at the young girl's halter, because there is no fence in their heart, nor knowledge of the one who varies the appearance of his creatures. The dew is not dew that has not been petitioned. Raise a million filters and the rain will not be clean, until the longing for it be refined in deep confession. And still we hear, If only this nation had a soul, or, Let us change the way we trade, or, Let us be proud of our region.

31

W HEN I HAVE NOT RAGE
or sorrow, and you depart from me, then I am most
afraid. When the belly is full, and the mind has its say-
ings, then I fear for my soul; I rush to you as a child at
night breaks into its parents' room. Do not forget me in
my satisfaction. When the heart grins at itself, the
world is destroyed. And I am found alone with the
husks and the shells. Then the dangerous moment

comes: I am too great to ask for help. I have other hopes. I legislate from the fortress of my disappointments, with a set jaw. Overthrow this even terror with a sweet remembrance: when I was with you, when my soul delighted you, when I was what you wanted. My heart sings of your longing for me, and my thoughts climb down to marvel at your mercy. I do not fear as you gather up my days. Your name is the sweetness of time, and you carry me close into the night, speaking consolations, drawing down lights from the sky, saying, See how the night has no terror for one who remembers the Name.

32

We cry out for what we have lost, and we remember you again. We look for each other, we cannot find us, and we remember you. From the ground of no purpose our children accuse us, and we remember, we recall a purpose. Could it be? we wonder. And here is death. Could it possibly be? And here is old age. And we never knew; we never stood up, and the good land was taken from us, and the sweet family was crushed. Maybe, we said, it could be, and we gave it a place among the possibilities. I'll do it myself, we said, as shame thickened the faculties of the heart. And the first reports were of failure, and the second of mutilations, and the third of every abomination. We remember, we cry out to you to return our soul. Is it really upon us? Yes, it is upon us. Do we merit this? Yes, we merit this. We cry out for what we have lost, and we remember you. We remember the containing word, the holy channels of commandment, and goodness waiting forever on the Path. And here and there, among the seventy tongues and the hundred darknesses – something, something shining, men of courage strengthening themselves to kindle the lights of repentance.

33

You who question souls, and you to whom souls must answer, do not cut off the soul of my son on my account. Let the strength of his childhood lead him to you, and the joy of his body stand him upright in your eyes. May he discern my prayer for him, and to whom it is uttered, and in what shame. I received the living waters and I held them in a stagnant pool. I was taught but I did not teach. I was loved but I did not love. I weakened the name that spoke me, and I chased the light with my own understanding. Whisper in his ear. Direct him to a place of learning. Illuminate his child's belief in mightiness. Rescue him from those who want him with no soul, who have their channels in the bedrooms of the rich and poor, to draw the children into death. Let him see me coming back. Allow us to bring forth our souls together to make a place for your name. If I am too late, redeem my yearning in his heart, bless him with a soul that remembers you, that he may uncover it with careful husbandry. They who wish to devour him have grown powerful on my idleness. They have a number for him, and a chain. Let him see them withered in the light of your name. Let him see their dead kingdom from the mountain of your word. Stand him up upon his soul, bless him with the truth of manhood.

34

You are with me still. Even though I have been removed, and my place does not recognize me. Even though I have filled my heart with stones. And my beloved says, *I will wait a little while behind this curtain – no, I have waited too long.* You are with me still. Though I scorched away the tears of return in the forced light of victory, your rebuke still comforts me, you signify yourself among the dangers. Saying, *Use this fear to know me, fix this exile toward my return.* Though I am unwept, it is your judgement parches me. Though my praises for you are under ban, it is the balance of your mercy. And you are with me still. Saying, *Search this out, it is you who have hidden yourself.* Saying, *Clear me in your troubled heart.* Saying, *I will come to you.* Saying, *I am here.* Though I add membrane to membrane against your light, and heap up cities on the husk of your rebuke, when the sun and the moon are shining in the other pan, and you advance me through the solitude by such a kind degree, and you create the world before my eyes, and the one who hides in self-disgrace cannot say Amen, O slow to anger, you are with me, you are with me still.

35

I TURNED YOU TO STONE.
You stepped outside the stone. I turned you to desire.
You saw me touch myself. I turned you into a tradition.
The tradition devoured its children. I turned you to
loneliness, and it corrupted into a vehicle of power. I
turned you into a silence which became a roar of accus-
ation. If it be your will, accept the longing truth be-
neath this wild activity. Open me, O heart of truth, hol-
low out the stone, let your Bride fulfil this loneliness. I
have no other hope, no other moves. This is my offer-
ing of incense. This is what I wish to burn, my darkness
with no blemish, my ignorance with no flaw. Bind me
to your will, bind me with these threads of sorrow, and
gather me out of the afternoon where I have torn my
soul on twenty monstrous altars, offering all things but
myself.

36

THOUGH I DON'T BELIEVE,
I come to you now, and I lift my doubt to your mercy.
Under the scorn of my own pride I open my mouth to
ask you again: Make an end to these harsh prepara-
tions. I made a crown for myself with your blessings,
and you locked me down to self-mockery. You said,
'Study the world that is without me, this wild degree of
solitude.' I covered up the path of desire and I over-
threw the bridge of tears, and I prepared the wilderness

on which the Accuser walks. The Accuser has no song, and he has no tears. Speak to me again. Speak to my words. Give this ghost the form of tears, that he move from nothing to sorrow, into Creation, even winter, even loss, that he have weight, that he be placed. Discover him in tears and make a place for his longing. Behold him in your court, one who upholds the throne of praises. Where have I been? I gave the world to the Accuser. Where do I go? I go to ask for pardon from the Most High.

37

IT IS ALL AROUND ME, THE darkness. You are my only shield. Your name is my only light. What love I have, your law is the source, this dead love that remembers only its name, yet the name is enough to open itself like a mouth, to call down the dew, and drink. O dead name that through your mercy speaks to the living name, mercy harkening to the will that is bent toward it, the will whose strength is its pledge to you – O name of love, draw down the blessing of completion on the man whom you have cut in half to know you.

38

As my fathers wrote, as my mothers spoke, to be so blessed as to know your name. Not far from here, where Rashi taught, to lift my voice in open thought. Beside the church where we were struck to prove some point on Christmas Eve, to be here still with broken heart and joyous word. To have this work, to fill this line, to be so blessed for my mother's sake, for my father's wine

39

FROM YOU ALONE TO YOU alone, everlasting to everlasting, all that is not you is suffering, all that is not you is solitude rehearsing the arguments of loss. All that is not you is the man collapsing against his own forehead, and the forehead crushes him. All that is not you goes out and out, gathering the voices of revenge, harvesting lost triumphs far from the real and necessary defeat. It is to you I speak, solitude to unity, failure to mercy, and loss to the light. It is you I welcome here, coming through the coarse glory of my imagination, to this very night, to this very couch, to this very darkness. Grant me a forgiving sleep, and rest my enemy.

40

Let me not pretend you are with me, when you are not with me. Let me close down, let the puppet fall among the strings, until, by your mercy, he rises as a man. Let him dare to call on you from the dust, when there is nothing but dust, and the coils of his defeat. Enter me again into the judgement, I who refuse to be judged. Enter me into the mercy, I who have forgotten mercy. Let me raise your kingdom to the beauty of your name. Why do you welcome me? asks the bitter heart. Why do you comfort me? asks the heart that is not broken enough. Let him lie among the strings until there is no hope for his daily strategy, until he cries, I am yours, I am your creature. Then the surface of the world is restored, then he can walk and build a will. Blessed are you whose blessings are discerned by those who know your name. The evil are seen clearly, and the good are beyond safety, and in the panic the whole world prays, Let us not be tested. Blessed are you who creates and destroys, who sits in judgement on numberless worlds, who judges the present with mercy.

41

I LOOK FAR, I FORGET YOU and I'm lost. I lift my hands to you. I kneel toward my heart. I have no other home. My love is here. I end the day in mercy that I wasted in despair. Bind me to you, I fall away. Bind me, ease of my heart, bind me to your love. Gentle things you return to me, and duties that are sweet. And you say, I am in this heart, I and my name are here. Everywhere the blades turn, in every thought the butchery, and it is raw where I wander; but you hide me in the shelter of your name, and you open the hardness to tears. The drifting is to you, and the swell of suffering breaks toward you. You draw me back to close my eyes, to bless your name in speechlessness. Blessed are you in the smallness of your whispering. Blessed are you who speaks to the unworthy.

42

It is to you I turn. The table stands on tiptoe. Every object leaps to its place. The closed book rises on its thousand pages and my wakefulness rejoices. I turn to you, my song in the house of night, my shield against the quarrels. I turn to you, who unifies the upward heart. Your name is the foundation of the night. The Accuser, with his thousand voices, stands in the place you are not named. Blessed is the name that holds this house in the firmness of mercy, and binds this song to the rock.

43

Holy is your name, holy is your work, holy are the days that return to you. Holy are the years that you uncover. Holy are the hands that are raised to you, and the weeping that is wept to you. Holy is the fire between your will and ours, in which we are refined. Holy is that which is unredeemed, covered with your patience. Holy are the souls lost in your unnaming. Holy, and shining with a great light, is every living thing, established in this world and covered with time, until your name is praised forever.

44

The meditations of the great are above me, and the entwining of the letters is beyond my skill. I cannot climb down to the vehicles of holiness, and my dreams do not ascend. But you have taught the heart to search itself in simple ways, with broom and rag, and you do not abandon my heart to the dust. I come to you for mercy and you hear my cry, and you shelter me in my portion, and you make my deeds a warning. Blessed are you who hears the cry of each man's portion. You cast me away to draw me back, you darken every expectation which is not you. You have taught me with a voice, you have rebuked me with a cheap reward. I cry from my defeat and you straighten my thought. It is your name that makes the cry a healing, it is your mercy that guards the heart in the panic of yes and no. Let the heart speak to its friend, you who decipher the world to a child. Let the heart speak of the love that humbles it for wilder love, and let my whispered gratitude uphold me through this day. In the hopelessness of every other thing, you make your place, you strengthen your presence, and I ask to bow down before the lord of my life.

45

NOT KNOWING WHERE TO go, I go to you. Not knowing where to turn, I turn to you. Not knowing how to speak, I speak to you. Not knowing what to hold, I bind myself to you. Having lost my way, I make my way to you. Having soiled my heart, I lift my heart to you. Having wasted my days, I bring the heap to you. The great highway covered with debris, I travel on a hair to you. The wall smeared with filth, I go through a pinhole of light. Blocked by every thought, I fly on the wisp of a remembrance. Defeated by silence, here is a place where the silence is more subtle. And here is the opening in defeat. And here is the clasp of the will. And here is the fear of you. And here is the fastening of mercy. Blessed are you, in this man's moment. Blessed are you, whose presence illuminates outrageous evil. Blessed are you who brings chains out of the darkness. Blessed are you, who waits in the world. Blessed are you, whose name is in the world.

46

HELP ME IN THE RAIN, help me in the darkness, help me at my aimless table. Bend me down to the rain, and let the darkness speak to my heart. Blessed are you who speaks from the darkness, who gives a form to desolation. You draw back the heart that is spilled in the world, you establish the borders of pain. Your mercy you make known to those who know your name, and your healing is discovered beneath the lifted cry. The ruins signal your power; by your hand it is broken down, and all things crack that your throne be restored to the heart. You have written your name on the chaos. The eyes that roll down the darkness, you have rolled them back to the skull. Let each man be sheltered in the fortress of your name, and let each one see the other from the towers of your law. Create the world again, and stand us up, as you did before, on the foundation of your light.

47

My soul finds its place in the Name, and my soul finds its ease in the embrace of the Name. I struggled with shapes and with numbers, and I carved with blade and brain to make a place, but I could not find a shelter for my soul. Blessed is the Name which is the safety of the soul, the spine and the shield of the innermost man, and the health of the innermost breath. I search the words that attend your mercy. You lift me out of destruction, and you win me my soul. You gather it out of the unreal by the power of your name. Blessed is the Name that unifies demand, and changes the seeking into praise. Out of the panic, out of the useless plan, I awaken to your name, and solitude to solitude all your creatures speak, and through the inaccessible intention all things fall gracefully. Blessed in the shelter of my soul, blessed is the form of mercy, blessed is the Name.

48

AWAKEN ME, LORD, FROM the dream of despair, and let me describe my sin. I would not fall into the bewilderment to which your name invited me. I established a court, and I fell asleep under a crown, and I dreamed I could rule the wicked. Awaken me to the homeland of my heart where you are worshipped forever. Awaken me to the mercy of the breath which you breathe into me. Remove your creature's self-created world, and dwell in the days that are left to me. Dissolve the lonely dream which is the judgement on my ignorance, and sweep aside the work of my hands, the barricades of uncleanliness, which I commanded against the torrents of mercy. Let your wisdom fill my solitude, and from the ruin raise your understanding. Blessed is the name of the glory of your kingdom forever and ever. What I have not said, give me the courage to say. What I have not done, give me the will to do. It is you, and you alone who refines the heart, you alone who instructs mortals, who answers the trembling before you with wisdom. Blessed is the name of the one who keeps faith with those who sleep in the dust, who has saved me again and again. To you is the day, and the conscious night, to you alone the only consecration. Bind me, intimate, bind me to your wakefulness.

49

ALL MY LIFE IS BROKEN unto you, and all my glory soiled unto you. Do not let the spark of my soul go out in the even sadness. Let me raise the brokenness to you, to the world where the breaking is for love. Do not let the words be mine, but change them into truth. With these lips instruct my heart, and let fall into the world what is broken in the world. Lift me up to the wrestling of faith. Do not leave me where the sparks go out, and the jokes are told in the dark, and new things are called forth and appraised in the scale of the terror. Face me to the rays of love, O source of light, or face me to the majesty of your darkness, but not here, do not leave me here, where death is forgotten, and the new thing grins.

50

I LOST MY WAY, I FORGOT
to call on your name. The raw heart beat against the
world, and the tears were for my lost victory. But you
are here. You have always been here. The world is all
forgetting, and the heart is a rage of directions, but
your name unifies the heart, and the world is lifted into
its place. Blessed is the one who waits in the traveller's
heart for his turning.

INDEX OF OPENING PHRASES

After searching among the words 4
All my life is broken unto you 49
As my fathers wrote, as my mothers spoke 38
Awaken me, Lord, from the dream of despair 48

Blessed are you who, among the numberless 14
Blessed are you who has given each man 9
Bless the Lord, O my soul 29

Did we come for nothing 17

Friend, when you speak this carefully 13
From you alone to you alone 39

He came back from his prayer 11
Help me in the rain, help me in the darkness 46
Here the destruction is subtle 30
Holy is your name, holy is your work 43

I draw aside the curtain 12
I heard my soul singing behind a leaf 3
I look far, I forget you and I'm lost 41
I lost my way, I forgot to call on your name 50
In the eyes of men he falls 8
In the thin light of hunted pleasure 24
I pushed my body from one city to another 7
Israel, and you who call yourself Israel 27
I stopped to listen, but he did not come 1
It is all around me, the darkness 37
It is to you I turn 42
I turned you to stone 35

Let me not pretend you are with me 40
'Let me rest,' he cried 5
Like an unborn infant swimming 20

My sister and I being estranged   23
My son and I lived in a cave   25
My soul finds its place in the Name   47
My teacher gave me what I do not need   21

Not knowing where to go, I go to you   45

Return, spirit, to this lowly place   16

Sit down, Master, on this rude chair   6
Sit in a chair and keep still   26

The meditations of the great are above me   44
They know me at this café   18
This is the way we summon one another   15
Though I don't believe, I come to you now   36

We cry out for what we have lost   32
When I have not rage or sorrow   31
When I left the king   2

You are with me still   34
You have sweetened your word on my lips   10
You let me sing, you lifted me up   19
Your cunning charlatan is trying   22
You who pour mercy into hell   28
You who question souls   33

Dominique Isserman

Leonard Cohen was born in Montreal in 1934. His poetry, novels, and songs are known around the world.